A PET FOR YOU
animal
hospital

with Rolf Harris

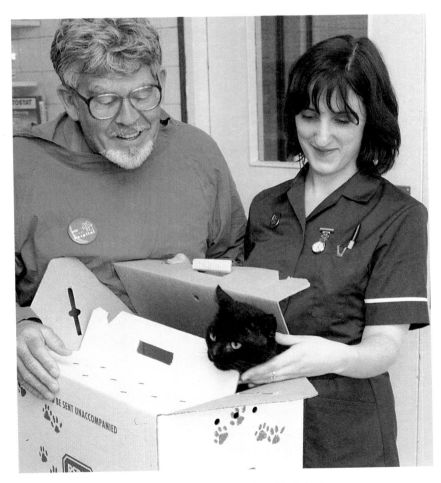

BBC BOOKS

Picture Acknowledgments

Bruce Coleman Limited: Hans Reinhard pps 23 (below), 34, 35, 38 (right), 40 (both). Carol Hunt p 37. RSPCA Photolibrary: pps 25 (below), 33 (below); Valerie Bissland p 29 (above); Colin Carver p 10 (left), p 42; Steve Cobb p 3; Robin Culley p 21; K Cutmore p 23 (above); Sean Dillow pps 25 (above), 30 (left), 46 (right); Stuart Harrop p 45 (left); Heritage Photography pps 14 (right), 19 (below right); A Holman p 33 (above); E A Janes pps 19 (above right), 24, 28, 36, 39, 44, 45 (right); Ian Jackson p 20; Geoff Langan pps 5 (above), 18; Mr and Mrs RP Lawrence pps 19 (left), 38 (left); Andrew Linscott pps 15, 30 (right); Ken McKay p 16 (below); Julie Meech p 32; D Muscroft p 26; Nigel Rolstone p 46 (left); Tim Sambrook pps 13 (below), 14 (left); Colin Seddon pps 8, 13 (above), 16 (above), 43; C Whyman p 11. Wayland Picture Library p 22. Tim Wainwright: Front and back cover, pps 1, 4 (both), 5 (below), 6 (both), 7, 9, 10 (right), 12, 17, 27, 29 (below), 31, 41, 47 (both), 48.

A donation of 15 pence is made
to the RSPCA for each copy of this book sold.

Text by Sarah Hargreaves, Producer of *Animal Hospital*

BBC Books wishes to thank the staff, patients and their owners at the RSPCA Harmsworth Hospital for their help in the production of this book.

The Executive Producer of *Animal Hospital* is Lorraine Heggessey

Published by BBC Children's Books
a division of BBC Worldwide Publishing Ltd
Woodlands, 80 Wood Lane, London W12 0TT

First published in 1995

Text, specially-commissioned photography and design © BBC Children's Books 1995

ISBN 0 563 40468 X

Typeset by BBC Children's Books
Printed by Cambus Limited, East Kilbride
Bound by Hunter & Foulis, Edinburgh
Cover printed by Clays Ltd, St Ives plc

Contents

Welcome to the Animal Hospital

We never know what sort of animal will come through the doors next when we're filming at the RSPCA's Animal Hospital in North London. It's true, most of the patients do have four legs and a tail, but not all. Some of them fly in, some hop or scuttle, and a few of them even slither. Usually pets are brought by their owners, but sometimes they are rushed in by RSPCA ambulances for emergency surgery. One or two are even escorted to the hospital by the police!

One little budgie was found down a drunk's trousers when he was arrested after a New Year party. The police brought the poor bird straight to the Animal Hospital. Although it sounds funny, he was in a sorry state. But the story had a happy ending. After a couple of days of loving care from the nurses here, the little fella was chirpy enough to go off to a happy new home.

▶ Rolf lends a hand with preparing one of the operating theatres.

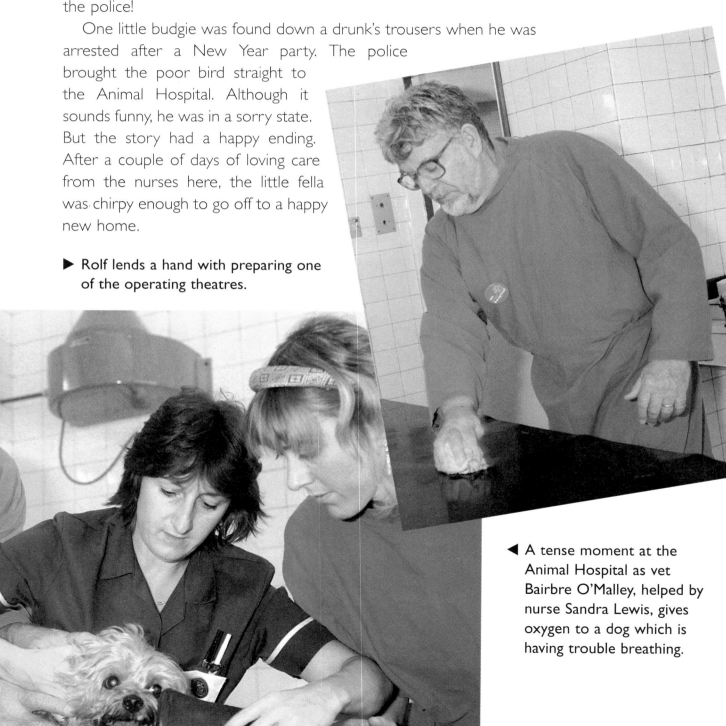

◀ A tense moment at the Animal Hospital as vet Bairbre O'Malley, helped by nurse Sandra Lewis, gives oxygen to a dog which is having trouble breathing.

Deciding to get a pet – and perhaps to adopt one like that budgie from the RSPCA – is the easy bit. But finding out what kind of animal is right for you is much trickier. There's a big difference between looking after a mouse and taking care of a Great Dane. What sort of pet would be right for you? Where should you get it from? How will you look after it from day to day? These are just a few of the questions you must ask yourself. A pet will give you lots of love but, in return, it will rely on you to look after it through thick and thin.

We've learned a lot from seeing the way the dedicated vets and nurses at the Animal Hospital look after pets. We hope this book will give you some ideas about how to choose a pet – and some useful hints on how to keep your animal healthy and happy too.

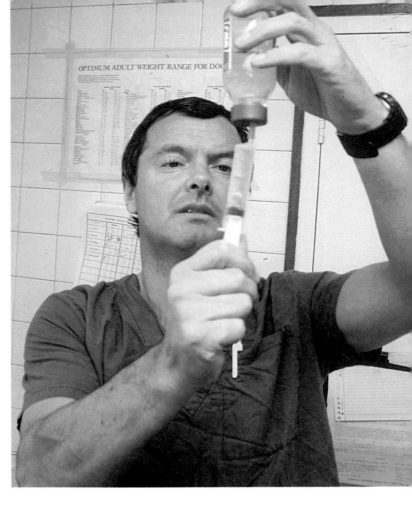

▲ Chief vet at the Harmsworth Memorial Animal Hospital is David Grant.

▼ Ouch! Rolf introduces David to a ticklish customer.

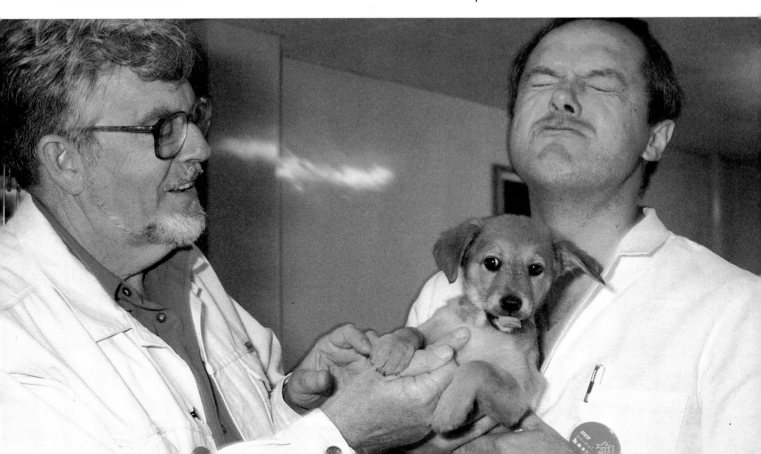

A Dog is For Life

All pets – cat, dog or goldfish – have one vital thing in common. They depend absolutely on their owner, not just for love, but for practical care and attention too. Sad to say, not all of them get these things, and sometimes the RSPCA has to step in to save an animal's life.

Snowy's Story

An RSPCA inspector received the emergency call to go to Tottenham Police Station. Waiting for him was a tiny bundle of skin and bones in a cardboard box – a little dog found abandoned and barely alive. Fearing the worst, the inspector rushed the small animal straight back to the Animal Hospital, where vet Bairbre O'Malley was on duty.

Bairbre couldn't contain her shock as the nurse lifted the pitiful creature on to the examination table. The dog could barely stand and her matted fur hung away from her sore, reddened skin. Her bones jutted painfully through the flesh. With horror, Bairbre discovered that this was a young animal, probably only two years old. Everyone who saw Snowy was horrified that anyone could treat a living creature so badly.

Even now that she's fully recovered, Snowy still has regular visits to the Animal Hospital to check for problems such as ear infections.

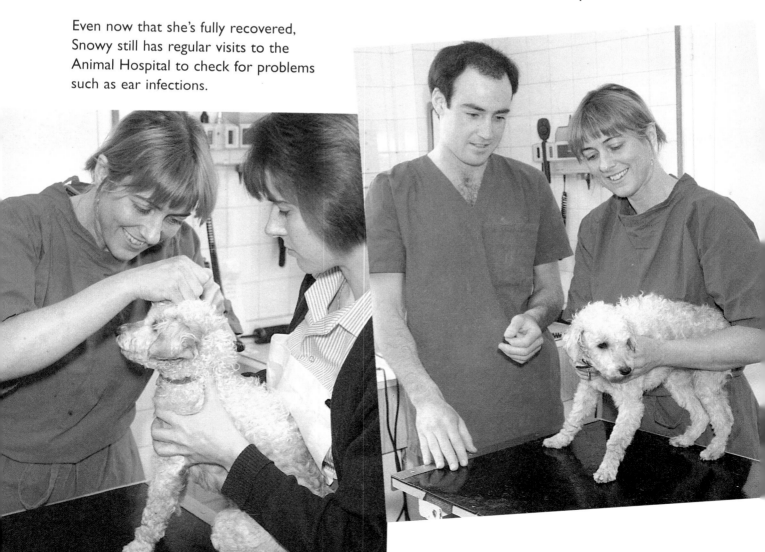

Snowy's new owner says that since she appeared on television, Snowy has become quite a celebrity. She is often recognized by fans when she's out having a walk!

Snowy was seriously malnourished and had scabies – a virulent skin disease – but astonishingly, Bairbre's tests revealed there was nothing wrong with the little dog that care and good food couldn't mend. Bairbre shaved off Snowy's dead fur. When she had finished she said that the dog looked "just like a little pink pig!" Snowy now began the slow process of recovery.

Snowy was taken in by foster carers who could provide the sort of individual, loving attention that she desperately needed. Animal Hospital viewers followed her progress over the weeks. The scabies was cured, the fur started to grow back and, most wonderful of all, Snowy started to respond to the love she was now being given. Today, she's a dog in a million.

Before You Buy a Dog . . .

Like Snowy, all dogs need love, but they also need attention every day of their life. Before you get a dog or puppy you have to ask yourself a few questions:

- Can you afford a dog? There are lots of costs to consider and, all in all, even a medium-sized dog can cost up to £1,000 a year.

- Can you look after a dog for all of its life? Remember, dogs often live up to fifteen years.

- Do you have a large enough home and a big enough garden?

- Do you have the time? Dogs should not be left alone for too long. They need company and lots of walks.

Dogs need exercise every day. Even if you are feeling tired, your pet will still have plenty of energy for its regular walk and play.

WHAT A DOG WILL COST

DOG FOOD
BETWEEN £200 AND £500 A YEAR (DEPENDING ON THE SIZE OF THE DOG)

VACCINATIONS
£40 A YEAR

NEUTERING
(AN OPERATION TO STOP YOUR DOG FROM BREEDING)
£100

VETS' BILLS
EVERY VISIT TO THE VET WILL BE AT LEAST £15. YOU CAN INSURE YOUR DOG AGAINST VETS' BILLS. IT COSTS ABOUT £80 PER YEAR.

A GOOD BASKET, COLLAR AND LEAD
£50

BOARDING FEES
IF YOU GO ON HOLIDAY, YOUR DOG MAY NEED TO GO INTO BOARDING KENNELS WHILE YOU ARE AWAY. THESE CAN COST UP TO £10 PER DAY.

Gypsy and Chips

Many people want to keep more than one pet. That's perfectly possible as long as you introduce the pets carefully so that they get on with one another.

Gypsy and Chips are great friends and stick together all the time. When the Chihuahua and the Yorkshire terrier first came to the Animal Hospital they were fearless, yapping at everyone and everything. Until they went in to see the vet, that is. Then, all their bravado evaporated. Suddenly, they were as good as gold!

The Right Dog For You

Dogs come in all shapes and sizes – which is handy because so do people and their homes!

At the Animal Hospital it isn't uncommon to see a massive Great Dane waiting patiently to see the vet, sitting next door to a pocket-sized Yorkie. Both dogs, but what a difference! If you get a dog, be careful to choose a breed that will suit you.

It's not just size you have to think about, either. Before you give a dog a home, find out about its temperament too. Big dogs aren't always the hardest to handle. On one occasion it took four people at the Animal Hospital, including Rolf, to hold a snappy little Pomeranian still while he had his stitches out.

▶ A Great Dane will need longer walks than a Chihuahua.

▲ If you buy a pure breed animal like this springer spaniel you can tell what the adult dog will look like while it is still a puppy.

Mongrels can be just as attractive as pure breeds, and every bit as healthy.

So which *is* the right dog for you?

- A big dog or a little dog? Remember, the bigger the dog, the more food and exercise it needs.

- A mongrel or a pure breed? With a breed you know exactly what you're getting, whether it will grow up to be big or small and what sort of temperament it is likely to have. However, some pedigree dogs are prone to inherited diseases or abnormalities which don't affect so many mongrels.

- If you're buying a puppy, try to see it with its mother to get a clear idea of its character. If that's not possible, pick a playful, outgoing puppy.

- If there are young children in your home, be sure to get a dog with a placid temperament. Train it to be loving and obedient, and remember that, just as your dog needs training, everyone else in your family will also need to be taught how to treat your pet.

Good Health For Dogs

You can't protect your dog from all illnesses, but you can certainly help keep it healthy by looking after it properly. Your vet will be able to give you advice when you first get a dog.

- Make sure your dog has annual injections against distemper, hepatitis, parvo virus, kennel cough and leptospirosis. These illnesses are very serious in dogs and can even kill.

- Make sure your dog is wormed regularly. Dogs may pick up roundworm or tapeworm and these can be treated easily.

- Unless you want to breed, get your dog neutered. This is a simple, painless operation which will stop your dog having puppies. You should not let your dog breed unless you are absolutely sure you will find good homes for all the pups.

- If your dog gets fleas, have it treated promptly by your vet, who will advise you on the best methods of treatment.

- Always keep your animal on a lead close to busy roads, and look out for hazards in the home, such as hot ovens and fires.

- Keep your pet clean by daily grooming and occasional baths.

- Make sure your dog's claws don't become overgrown. If they do get too long, they can be very painful and must be clipped. It's especially important to check the claws of older dogs.

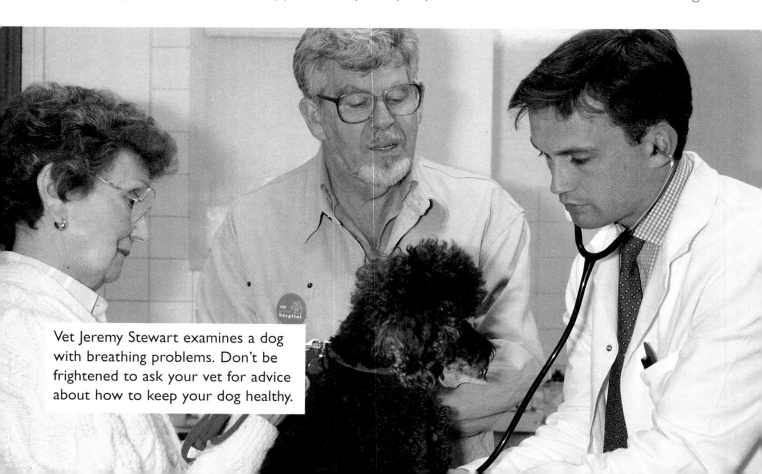

Vet Jeremy Stewart examines a dog with breathing problems. Don't be frightened to ask your vet for advice about how to keep your dog healthy.

Part of the RSPCA's work is in organizing information campaigns about animal safety. Dog safety belts are a good idea if your pet travels by car – and you should never leave your dog alone in a car.

Rocky's Manicure

One human year is the equivalent of seven dog years, so when Rocky, a twenty-year-old dog, came into vet Stan McCaskie's clinic, it took Rolf a minute or two to work out that this dog was 140 years old! No wonder that Rocky wanted to lie down on the examination table all the time. He was having trouble with his dew claws – the little extra claws that grow half-way up the legs of some dogs. They had become so overgrown that they were curled all the way around. Rocky was obviously in pain, but Stan soon cut the claws right back, cleaned up the leg and sent him on his way with a protective bandage.

Some breeds of dog need special care. Regular grooming is essential for a long-haired Old English sheepdog.

Strays

Often the staff arriving at the Animal Hospital for the early shift find a sad, abandoned dog dumped on the doorstep. They take it in and do what they can to find it a new home.

There are thousands and thousands of stray dogs, and they are a real problem.

Some strays have been deliberately turned out by owners who have grown tired of them. "It's particularly bad around Christmas time," says chief vet, David Grant. "I remember coming in one Monday morning just after New Year to find that ten stray dogs had been brought in that morning alone."

However, some strays have clearly been loved and cared for. They haven't been neglected – they've just got lost. Sometimes, their owners are searching desperately for them.

▼ Microchipping is a quick and painless way of tagging your dog.

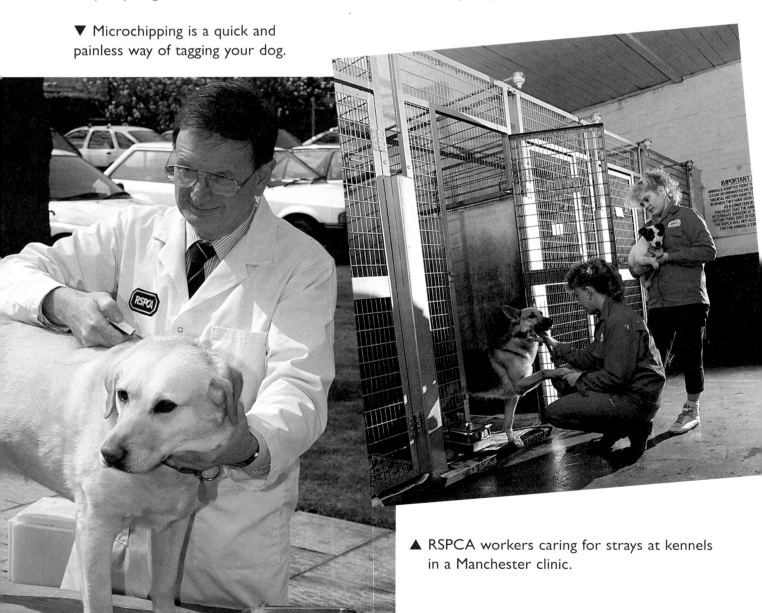

▲ RSPCA workers caring for strays at kennels in a Manchester clinic.

There's nothing sadder than a homeless young dog.

Losing a pet can be really distressing for both you and it, so you should do everything you can to identify it clearly. There are two main things you should do:

- Get your dog a sturdy collar. Put your name and address on it. The best type of name tags are engraved flat metal discs. Barrel-shaped tags are not as good because they can become unscrewed quite easily.

- Get your dog microchipped too. A microchip is a tiny silicon chip which a vet can implant, painlessly, under your dog's skin. The chip can be read with a special scanner and its number is kept on a national computer, along with the animal's name and address. If your pet ever gets lost, a quick scan will soon tell the RSPCA where it lives.

Training

If your dog won't do as it's told, you may soon get fed up with it. Your neighbours certainly will!

You'll need to spend some time training your dog to obey simple commands. The basics for it to learn are "Sit!" "Go Down!" "Come!" and "Stay!" A dog training class can be really helpful if you're not sure how to start teaching your pet, and there will be one somewhere near you.

▲ An obedient dog will give its owner much more pleasure than one which has never had any basic training.

▶ It's much easier to exercise a dog if it can obey basic commands.

Who said that you can't teach an old dog new tricks? Golden retriever Harvey is still learning. When he was 8 years old his owner, Richard Thompson, the nursing supervisor at the Animal Hospital, taught him to balance orange segments on his nose.

You must also teach your dog to be friendly with other dogs, and dog training classes are a good way of helping your pet to get used to other animals. At the Animal Hospital we met one dog called Digger who loved human beings but had a real problem with other dogs. Pretty soon, that became a problem for his owners too.

Digger

Digger had been the much-loved pet of an elderly man. When his owner had to go into an old people's home, Digger found himself looking for a new home too. He was a lovable chap and was quickly adopted, but then the trouble started. Digger just didn't like other dogs. Every time he went out for a walk he would bark furiously, and sometimes even try to attack. He'd never really got used to the company of other dogs because he had lived almost all of his life as a house dog. His new owners took him to dog training classes to try and teach him to mix with other dogs, but until he had learned to be friendly, he could never be let off the leash.

Before You Buy a Rabbit . . .

Rabbits always look irresistible in pet shops, don't they? And they *do* make very good pets, but like all animals, they need to be looked after carefully. If you decide to keep a rabbit, never forget that they are mute animals. Unlike a dog or a cat, they can't cry out for help if they're hungry or thirsty. They rely on you always to remember what they need.

What Rabbits Need . . .

- A good-sized hutch with a nest box, kept nice and clean. Your rabbit can live out of doors as long as its hutch is in a sheltered spot. You can use newspaper, sawdust, wood shavings, straw or hay to cover the floor of the hutch.

- Fresh food and water, twice a day. Special rabbit pellets are the best. You can also give your pet small quantities of carrots, cabbage or salad, but don't give your rabbit grass cuttings.

- Daily exercise. Rabbits should not sit in their hutch all the time.

- Company. Rabbits don't really like to be on their own. However, be careful that you do not keep a male and a female together or you'll soon have lots of babies.

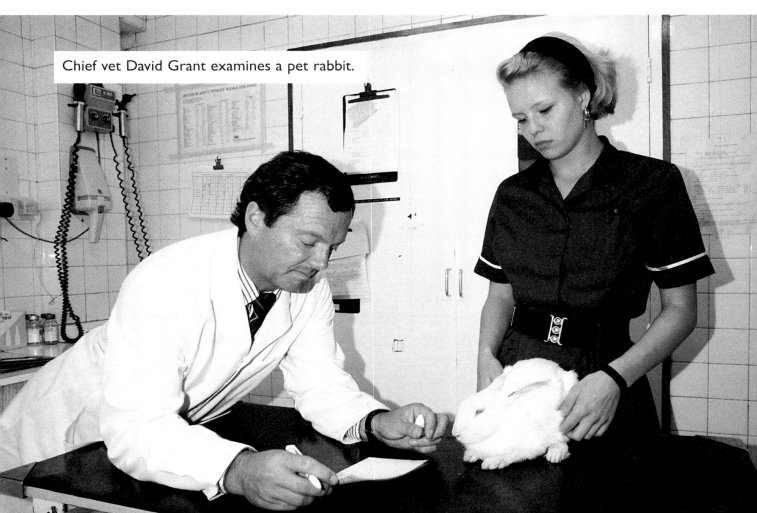

Chief vet David Grant examines a pet rabbit.

▶ *above* A chinchilla rabbit – one of the more unusual lop-eared breeds you can buy.

▶ *below* Two baby rabbits which were brought into an RSPCA clinic for treatment.

▼ Rabbits are sociable animals. They do not like to live alone.

Rabbits are usually healthy creatures, but you may still need to visit the vet from time to time.

Sooty

Sooty, a silky black rabbit, had a real problem. He just couldn't eat his carrots! Vet Jeremy Stewart soon discovered what was wrong. Sooty's bottom teeth didn't meet the top ones so they had nothing to grind them down. They had just grown and grown – until they were sticking a couple of centimetres out of his mouth. No wonder he couldn't chew! The solution was simple, even though it made Rolf wince. Jeremy took the clippers to Sooty's teeth and simply cut them back to size.

Run, Rabbit, Run – And How to Stop It

There are always rabbits in the miscellaneous ward at the Animal Hospital and they are almost all strays. It's a real problem for the RSPCA, who have more rabbits than they can cope with.

Owners often forget that rabbits are very good at burrowing. If a cage is not secure, any enterprising bunny can be off and away in no time. So if you fence in a bit of lawn as a rabbit run, make sure you put mesh on the ground too.

Rabbits who escape don't just become wild rabbits. If they've never lived in the wild they cannot survive away from home and often end up at an RSPCA rehoming centre.

Chas

Chas is the sort of rabbit you see in story books. Small and brown, with a white bob tail and big soft eyes. But nobody wanted him. He'd been at the rehoming centre so long that when the next stray came in, Chas would have had to be put to sleep because there just wasn't enough room to keep him any more.

Fortunately he appeared on Animal Hospital in the nick of time, and a kind-hearted couple who already had several other rabbits in their garden gave him a loving home.

It's important to clean out your rabbit hutch regularly.

A hutch and a large, secure outdoor pen are the best kind of home for your rabbit.

Fish Can Be Fun

If you don't have a garden or a big home, perhaps you should think about keeping fish. Goldfish are the commonest cold water fish. If you don't have much room for a bigger animal, they can be ideal pets. However, never try to win a goldfish from a fair. Fairs are fun for you, but not for goldfish.

Goldfish need . . .

- A good-sized tank, regularly cleaned out and filled with fresh water. A tank with a filtration system to keep the water clean all the time is best. Before you buy your fish, you should ask for advice at a specialist shop.

- Plants and stones to give shelter.

- Daily feeding. A good brand of commercial fish food contains everything your fish needs.

- A friend. Fish enjoy having some company, just like people.

It's a good idea to watch carefully and see exactly how much your fish eats each time you feed it. That way, you can be sure that you don't overfeed your pet. Uneaten fish food quickly pollutes the tank.

Never bring home a goldfish from a fair on the spur of the moment. First get your fish tank ready. Then buy your goldfish from a good pet shop.

A Fishy Tale

One of the RSPCA inspectors at the Animal Hospital thought he was in for an easy morning when he got a call to go to pick up a few goldfish from an old lady who was unable to look after them any more. But when he got there, he discovered she had more than *thirty* assorted fish, and now they all needed new homes. After some head scratching, he took the easy option. They went into the hospital's own pond.

Before You Buy a Cat . . .

Cats are often easy-going, independent pets. But don't believe that old saying about them having nine lives. If you choose a cat for a pet, you've got to look after it very carefully.

Your cat will like a snug, private basket where it can take naps.

You will need . . .

- Somewhere cosy and private for your cat to sleep.

- Food every day. Cats can be fussy eaters, and you may need to vary their food until you find out what they really like. Good quality tinned food is best.

- Fresh water every day. In spite of what most people think, milk isn't always good for cats. It can give some of them diarrhoea.

- Quite a lot of money. Cats are not as expensive as dogs, but they still cost around £500 a year to keep, and can live for up to 15 years or more.

- A cat flap set into the door or window of your home, so that your cat can come and go as it pleases (as long as you do not live on a busy main road).

- A litter tray, cleaned out regularly.

WHAT WILL A CAT COST?

FOOD — ABOUT £200 PER YEAR

NEUTERING (AN OPERATION TO STOP YOUR CAT HAVING BABIES) — ABOUT £50

VACCINATIONS — ABOUT £30 PER YEAR

VETS' BILLS — AT LEAST £15 PER VISIT PLUS THE COST OF THE MEDICINES

CAT LITTER — £35

A GOOD QUALITY **BASKET** AND **COLLAR** — £20

◀ Good-quality cat food is the best diet for your cat.

A Surprise Haircut

Animals often have to be anaesthetised, not just for operations, but even for quite simple procedures. When a marmalade-coloured Persian cat came into the Animal Hospital with very matted fur, vet Stan McCaskie immediately booked him in for an anaesthetic.

The cat went off to sleep happily enough, little knowing what he would wake up to. In fact, he was off to the barber! His fur was so badly matted it had to be almost all shaved off. When he came round he saw that he had a mohican haircut – just a crest of fur left along his back and head – and he slunk off into the corner of the cage to hide his blushes!

▶ Cats are independent animals and like to come and go as they please.

Choosing the Right Kind of Cat

Any cat owner will be able to pick their cat out from hundreds of others – all cats are individuals. There are smooth-haired cats, long-haired cats, moggies and pedigrees, and they can have very different personalities. You may find, as one owner who visited the Animal Hospital, that you have a cat who needs rather special attention.

Oscar

We first met Oscar when he came to have his leg examined. He had been run over by a car. At first it had seemed that he might lose the leg, but cats are remarkable for the way that even serious wounds can heal. Oscar was soon up and walking again.

Oscar's real difficulty is that he is deaf. However, his owner has found all kinds of ingenious ways of overcoming this problem. She has taught him sign language, and if he can see her, he will respond to her hand movements. If he's out late at night, she flashes the garden light twice and he knows that it's time to come in to bed. And if he's somewhere in the house, his owner stamps twice on the floor – Oscar feels the vibrations and comes running down for dinner.

Most cats look after themselves pretty well, but some do need quite a bit of attention. Long-haired cats need regular grooming to stop their coats getting matted.

Rolf with Oscar, now fully recovered after his accident.

Keeping Your Cat Healthy

As with dogs, you can save your cat from many illnesses by simple, regular care. Your local vet will always be able to give you advice on how to prevent your pet from becoming sick.

- Starting at the age of nine weeks, make sure your cat has injections once a year against cat flu and enteritis. Both of these common illnesses can kill. Your cat can also be vaccinated against the leukaemia virus.

- Worm your cat regularly. Worms are a common problem in cats, but they can easily be avoided.

- Have your cat treated promptly if it gets fleas.

- Be careful what you feed to your cat. Never give it cooked bones as they can easily get stuck in a cat's throat.

- Beware of hazards about your home. Cats are curious creatures, and hot ovens and fires can be dangerous.

Curious Kitten

Curiosity almost got the better of one little cat who came into the Animal Hospital. According to chief vet David Grant, this was the most unusual case he had ever had to deal with. The little black kitten was rushed into hospital covered in a sticky wax. He had leapt from a bed and landed straight in a pot of melted leg wax prepared by his owner. The wax couldn't be shaved off because it had stuck to his skin as well as his fur.

It took several careful treatments with strong washing-up liquid and surgical spirit before Phoenix was clean and fluffy again and ready to go home.

Young cats will investigate anything that catches their attention.

▲ Generally speaking, cats are good at keeping themselves clean, but you should inspect your pet regularly for any signs of worms or fleas.

Itchy Pets

One morning, a group of young women students who shared a house presented themselves at the Animal Hospital. Rather sheepishly, one of them admitted that they had been sent down to the hospital by their doctor, who suspected that they had all caught ringworm from their two Persian cats. They were feeling very itchy!

A quick examination of the red, circular marks on one student's neck and an ultra-violet scan for the cats proved that the doctor was quite right about the illness.

The treatment for ringworm is quite simple, but it can take up to three months to work. So there would be no more cuddles for these cats until they were well and truly cured!

▶ Vet Jeremy Stewart prepares Spot for an injection. Spot belongs to a member of the Animal Hospital's nursing staff.

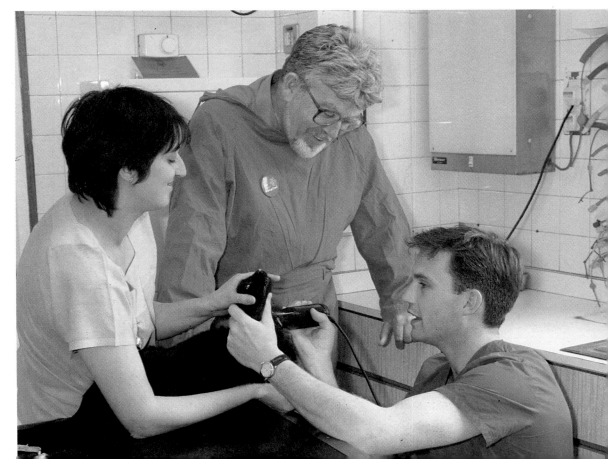

Cats and Kittens

Tiny kittens may look cute and irresistible but the sad truth is that there are far too many cats in the world and not enough good owners to care for them. You should have your cat neutered at the first possible opportunity. Neutering is a simple, painless operation which will prevent your cat from having kittens.

Finding a good home for unwanted kittens is not easy, and many are brought in to the RSPCA every week. One young woman brought a four-week old kitten into the Animal Hospital. Two men had been offering it for sale in a pub the night before. The young woman felt so sorry for the kitten that she had bought it there and then – but buying a kitten in a pub is not a good way of getting a pet and no small animal should be treated in this way.

▶ Newly-born kittens should not be separated from their mothers until they are at least eight weeks old.

◀ This couple have just picked up a new pet from an RSPCA rehoming centre.

These two slippery characters were waiting for new owners when they attached themselves to Rolf.

If you decide that you would like to have a cat as a pet, you will find many kittens waiting at RSPCA rehoming centres for someone to choose them. Don't ignore the adult cats looking for new homes either. They can make lovely pets too.

Keeping Tabs on Your Tabby

There are two things you should do to prevent your cat from getting lost.

- Buy your cat a good collar with your name and address on it. Make sure that the collar has elastic in it, so that it will come off easily if it gets caught on something. Lots of cats are brought into the Animal Hospital because they have been trapped by collars which are not elasticated.

- Have your cat fitted with a microchip by your local vet. Just as with dogs, a silicon chip can be inserted painlessly under the cat's skin. If the cat gets lost, the number can be read with a special scanner and its details looked up on a national computer.

Stray cats are always being brought into the hospital. Without a collar or a chip, there's little chance they'll ever be reunited with their owners. Just occasionally, they're lucky.

All cats are special to their owners, so if you've got one, make sure it doesn't get lost.

Zag's X-Ray

One Animal Hospital programme featured all the stray cats that are brought in to the hospital. We filmed a little cat being taken to a rehoming centre. The very next day the telephone rang. It was a woman who lived in Hastings in Kent, more than 70 miles away. She was positive that the cat she'd seen on television was hers. She had lost her six months before and had given up all hope of ever seeing her pet again.

Zag had lived on a caravan site in Hastings and she must have hitched a lift to London in the boot of a camper's car. She had tried to go off for a ride before, but previously someone had always spotted her before it was too late.

▲ It's in a cat's nature to go exploring, so don't let your pet out of doors without a collar and identification tag.

Even after six months, her owner had no doubts that this was her cat, and she could prove it. She had some X-rays of Zag's leg which had been taken after an earlier road accident. They matched exactly X-rays taken of the stray in London. Zag and her owner were soon reunited, but not before she had been microchipped in case she ever gets wanderlust again.

◄ Every year the RSPCA takes in many well cared-for cats which have strayed from home, but are wearing no kind of identification.

33

Before You Buy a Hamster . . .

Of all rodents, hamsters are the most popular pets, but don't believe anyone who tells you that they are sleepy little creatures. They do like to snooze during the day, but at night there's no stopping them! It has been calculated that in the wild they walk five miles every night. They groom and gnaw, they climb and play. Pet hamsters are constantly rearranging their cages. What's more, if you're not careful, they will also escape. Any hamster cage must be strong and carefully made because hamsters are the best escape artists around.

Multiplying Hamsters

Offering to look after a friend's hamster is not always a good idea. It's particularly dangerous if the visitor is a male and yours is a female.

"They met for just five minutes, in the bathroom!" wailed a young owner as she and her friend put down three boxes of hamsters in front of vet David Grant. She had taken care of her friend's pet for a few days, and now, instead of only one hamster, there were so many babies that she had ten animals to look after.

The little hamsters had a bowel infection which was making them very sick indeed. Two of them had to be admitted to the Animal Hospital for special care, and the others were given antibiotics to put in their water.

David also warned the girls that they must separate the male and female babies quickly. At seven or eight weeks, they would start to breed themselves. So, if they were left together, instead of nine babies, they would have . . . well, work it out for yourself!

◀ An open hamster wheel is a good way for your pet to get plenty of exercise without it ever even leaving its cage.

Hamsters come in all sorts of colours, but the most common is the golden hamster.

Hamsters need . . .

- A good strong cage, with places to run and hide. Modern plastic cages are warmer than metal ones, and are safer than wooden cages because hamsters cannot gnaw through the plastic.

- Bedding and floor covering. Put sawdust or peat on the base of the cage and use white paper or tissue for the nest. Do not put paper printed with coloured ink in the cage, as it can poison your pet.

- Fresh food and water every day. Special hamster pellets provide a balanced diet, and can be supplemented with small amounts of fresh fruit, vegetables and nuts.

- Toys and things to gnaw. Hard dog biscuits are ideal.

- Grooming. Long-haired hamsters need special care. Comb them with a soft toothbrush.

- No company. Never try to keep more than one hamster in the same cage. Hamsters like to live alone and will attack other hamsters, even their brothers and sisters.

Gerbils

Gerbils are another kind of rodent which make good pets.

Gerbils need . . .

- A good-sized home. This could be a large glass tank, filled with peat moss for the gerbils to burrow in and white paper for them to shred. You could also put wood shavings in the tank, but it's best to avoid artificial materials, especially ones with long fibres that can become tangled around little legs. The gerbil tank must be kept indoors and be cleaned out regularly.

- Fresh food and water every day. You can buy specially-prepared mice or rat diets at good pet shops, and these are suitable for gerbils too. In addition, you might want to give your gerbil sunflower seeds and some fresh vegetables or salad, but don't feed them too much or you will upset their digestion. Gerbils are desert animals and do not drink a lot, but they still need fresh water every day.

Not all rodents are easy to look after. On the surface, you might not think there was much difference between keeping a chinchilla or a gerbil, but even though they look very appealing, chinchillas need much more specialist care. Do not be tempted to get one unless you really know how to look after it properly.

Gerbils like company and become unhappy if they live alone, but make sure that you only keep animals of the same sex together in the same cage. Gerbils can have up to 30 babies a year!

Charlie Chinchilla

Charlie's teeth had been giving him trouble for some time. He could not eat and was in pain, but did not want vet Jeremy Stewart to examine him. Every time Jeremy put a probe into the chinchilla's mouth, Charlie put up a tiny paw to stop it. Eventually Jeremy had to anaesthetize the pet in order to get a good look at the problem.

It can be dangerous to give anaesthetic to tiny animals, particularly nervous little creatures such as chinchillas. His owner was far from happy as Charlie disappeared into the treatment room. He was put into a specially-adapted water bottle which was then filled with gas. Vet Bairbre O'Malley quickly found the sharp back teeth which were causing Charlie such pain. She carefully filed them down, giving the pet extra doses of gas when he started to wake up. It was a tense time, but Charlie was soon back safe in the hands of his owner.

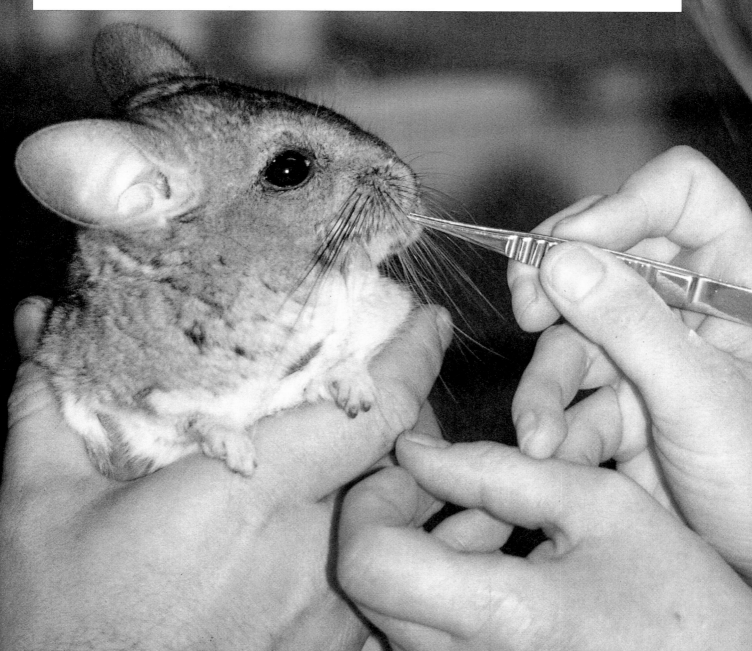

Mice and Rats

Mice are often kept as pets, but, perhaps surprisingly, rats can be good animals to keep too. If they are bred as pets, rats can be affectionate creatures, and contrary to their bad reputation, they rarely bite.

Both rats and mice are quite easy to keep and become very tame if they are handled regularly. However, you should not follow the example of one owner we met at the Animal Hospital. She liked to carry her pet rat, Poppy, around with her under her jumper. On one occasion when she was travelling home on the bus, Poppy poked her head out to take a look at the old lady sitting in the next seat. Well . . . you can imagine the rest!

Mice and rats need . . .

- A good-sized cage. Put wood shavings, straw or shredded white paper on the floor. It will need cleaning out two or three times a week. Like hamsters, mice and rats will gnaw anything, so wooden cages can be a problem.

- Regular feeding. Mice and rat food is available from good pet shops and contains everything your pet will need. If you want, you can also give it small amounts of foods such as apples, biscuits or tomatoes.

- Other mice or rats for company. However, as with all other rodents, do not mix the sexes.

▲ Although you should not go near rats in the wild, pet rats can be affectionate animals.

▶ White mice are the most popular variety to be kept as pets.

An old shoe box makes a snug winter nest for a wood mouse.

The Abandoned Mouse Mystery

One morning, a nurse arriving for the early shift at the hospital found a cage dumped on the doorstep. Inside were two white mice which had clearly been well cared for. With them was a little note, saying simply, "More to follow." No one knew quite what to make of it, but, like all waifs and strays, the mice were taken into the hospital to be checked over before being sent on to a rehoming centre. It would probably be fairly easy to find a new owner for two tiny mice.

However, when the early shift nurse clocked on the *next* morning, the meaning of the note became clear immediately. There were no longer just two white mice – there were eleven! One of them had been expecting babies.

Pet Birds

Budgerigars are the commonest pet birds, and they are the easiest to keep.

Budgies need . . .

- An aviary or good-sized cage. It should have at least two perches so that your bird can get some exercise by moving from perch to perch. Clean the cage out every week.

- Food and clean water every day. Special budgie food contains everything a budgie needs.

- Company. Your pet will need lots of human attention or another budgie as a companion.

- Daily exercise outside the cage.

- A cuttlefish to peck at. This way your budgie will be able to keep its beak short.

- Toys to play with. A mirror makes a good toy, and budgies that live on their own will often have long conversations with their own reflections!

Exotic Birds

Some people like to keep larger or more exotic birds, such as parrots or cockatoos. They do look beautiful, but beware – they are not easy animals to keep and they need a great deal of attention. Unless you have the experience and expertise, you should really stick to a simpler pet. If an exotic bird falls ill, you will also have to visit a vet with experience in treating it or even a specialist.

Mavis, another pet hen from the same flock as Geraldine.

Geraldine Hen

"This is Geraldine!" announced her owner, putting a large cardboard box down on to the clinic examining table. We knew *who* was in the box, but not *what*. As the lid came up, so did Geraldine's head. A long, thin feathered neck and two beady eyes peered round at Rolf and the cameras. Geraldine was a hen – not exactly an exotic bird, but certainly an unusual one to keep as a pet.

Geraldine's owner has a small flock of pet hens at the bottom of her garden. They are all retired battery hens. Geraldine had been brought to the hospital because some of her feathers were falling out. "She looks practically oven-ready!" lamented her owner, pointing out the bald patches to vet Jeremy Stewart.

Jeremy prescribed a course of medicine, but Geraldine would also have to be kept away from the other hens in case her disease was contagious.

"Oh well," sighed her owner. "She'll just have to live indoors with me for a while!"

Wild Birds

It is possible to keep wild birds or birds of prey as pets, but the RSPCA advises against it because they are very difficult to look after. Birds such as falcons can also be dangerous and should never be approached by anyone who does not know how to handle them.

Barney Barn Owl

One of the RSPCA's inspectors had to pick up a pet barn owl from a teenage boy called John. John had done all the right things. He had built a large enclosure and taken the owl out to fly every morning before he went off to school. But he still felt that life for Barney could be better and that perhaps he'd made a mistake in getting a barn owl as a pet.

While the inspector drew up the papers signing the owl over to the RSPCA, John said a last goodbye to Barney who sat happily on his shoulder, kissing his ear. It was clear that John would miss Barney, but Barney was going to miss John too.

Goodbyes over, Barney set off for a specialist owl sanctuary where he was to live for the rest of his days.

Barn owls are truly magnificent creatures, but it is very hard to give them everything they need to make them happy if they are kept as pets.

It is possible to hand feed fledglings like these blackbirds if they have been abandoned completely. However, most fledglings are best left somewhere safe where their real parents can find them again.

Fledglings

The little bundle of feathers was squeaking piteously, its beak wide open ready for food. The first blackbird fledgling of the year had arrived at the Animal Hospital. Nursing supervisor Richard Thompson was feeding it on a mixture of cat food and vitamins.

Although the hospital is really there to treat pets, in spring people sometimes bring in fledglings that they have found on the ground. Unfortunately, that's not always the best thing they can do for the baby birds.

"The trouble with this little bird," Richard told Rolf, "is that it thinks I'm its mum now!" Baby birds imprint their characters on the creature that feeds them, and this little blackbird now thought he was a human being!

Richard explained that the best thing to do with fledglings which have fallen out of their nest is to put them into an open-topped box on a window sill or garage roof. They must be in a place where they will be safe from predators. When the parents hear their baby, they will come and feed it until it can fend for itself.

Strange Visitors

Amongst all the dogs, cats, hamsters and budgerigars, the Animal Hospital also has more unusual visitors. Some of the rarities are tortoises.

Tortoises used to be quite common pets in Britain, but the climate does not really suit them, and it is now illegal to import them into the country. However, the vets and nurses still see them from time to time because they live for so long.

Toto and Charlie

Rolf helped the owner put her two big shopping bags on to the examination table. They were quite a weight. Then he looked on in amazement as she pulled out first one and then another enormous tortoise. Toto and Charlie had woken up from their long winter sleep but their owner was worried because she could not get them to eat. The time just after hibernation is sometimes a difficult one for tortoises.

Toto and Charlie were at least 28 years old. Their owner had removed them from two boys who had been hitting them against railings all those years ago. Toto still had a triangle of his shell missing where it had been smashed off by one of the boys.

Vet Stan McCaskie examined both of the tortoises thoroughly, although he needed some help from their owner to make them co-operate. He pronounced them to be generally in good health, but suggested a luke-warm bath to pep them up. They would soon be ready to face another year.

Tortoises can survive out of doors in Britain during the summer, but they are happiest in warmer countries.

Some people are fascinated by snakes or iguanas, but they are difficult animals to keep well as pets.

Reptiles

Snakes and other reptiles are very specialised pets and you should not keep them unless you have the knowledge and experience to look after them properly. They need carefully-controlled living conditions and a special diet.

Bart the Iguana

Bart was a spectacular green iguana, the kind of creature rarely seen outside a zoo. He needed an X-ray because one of his front toes was bent at an odd angle.

Rolf was keen to try out an old trick he'd heard about. If you stroke an iguana rhythmically on its breast bone, he said, it would be mesmerised and sit stock still. Vet Stan McCaskie was sceptical, but he prepared for the X-ray while Rolf practised mesmerising.

Bart, however, was having none of it. When he was put down on the X-ray table, he promptly ran off. Finally, Stan resorted to masking tape to stick Bart down to the table. Undignified for Bart, but effective.

Animals and You

The RSPCA knows that even when it saves a life, it never gets a "thank you". But that's the whole point. The animals that the Society helps can not speak up for themselves if they are suffering. They can't telephone for assistance or write to the newspapers, and they can never say "thank you" directly – though some animals, like Snowy, do manage to show their gratitude in other ways.

Every thirty seconds someone, somewhere in England and Wales contacts the RSPCA about an animal in need. Inspectors and ambulance drivers work around the clock, racing to answer emergency calls. They frequently face difficult and dangerous situations. They have to learn how to handle many different kinds of animal, and they are all trained in rock climbing and using a boat too. If there's a sheep trapped on a cliff ledge, a beached porpoise or even a cat stuck 20 metres up a tree, it's the RSPCA inspectors who go out to save them.

Some of the RSPCA's work is heart-rending. Cruelty to animals, whether deliberate or accidental, is hard to understand and it comes in many forms. In Snowy's case, it was easy to see. Extreme neglect soon reduces an animal to a terrible state. But what about someone who loves ponies so much that he decided to keep one in his little flat? Or another man who called in the RSPCA himself when he became concerned that his two pet sharks, kept in a tank in his seventh-floor tower-block flat, were getting too big!

▲ Finding new homes for stray or deserted animals is one part of the RSPCA's work.

▶ A cat at one of the RSPCA's animal shelters makes friends with a possible new owner.

All of these problems are brought along for the RSPCA to sort out. Many of the animals end up in RSPCA hospitals and rehoming centres, because no case is completed until the animal is found a new and suitable home.

In addition to the exciting, unusual and sometimes distressing work undertaken by the RSPCA, there is also the day-to-day task of educating people about animal welfare – everything from pet care to the transportation of live animals. In fact, wherever you find animals, you'll find the RSPCA. The Society visits pet shops, race courses, zoos and stables, monitoring the treatment of animals.

▼ Rolf and Harmsworth vet Stan McCaskie.

▲ Rolf with Gizmo who came into the Animal Hospital with a slipped disc but made a full recovery after an emergency operation.

It's all a huge job for the vets, nurses, inspectors and ambulance drivers. But the good news is that the RSPCA has one more essential worker – you. By looking after your own pets well, finding out about animal welfare and by reporting any suffering you see to the RSPCA, you'll be doing your own bit to help.

Of course, you can't expect a "thank you" – but if you're lucky, you might get a woof, a meow or a cheep-cheep!

47

This goat must be one of the most unusual strays ever to be brought in to the Animal Hospital. He was found in a park over a bank holiday. He had not been very well cared for, but chief vet David Grant hoped that, after a check up, he would find a new home on a city farm. In the meantime, the goat became great pals with Rolf.

Further information about how you can support the RSPCA and its work can be obtained from:
RSPCA Headquarters, Causeway, Horsham, West Sussex RH12 1HG
Anyone under the age of 17 can join the Animal Action Club
and become a junior member of the RSPCA.